D1135406

WITHDRAWN

THE
**PAUL HAMLYN
LIBRARY**

———•———

DONATED BY

THE PAUL HAMLYN

FOUNDATION

TO THE

BRITISH MUSEUM

———•———

opened December 2000

THE BRITISH MUSEUM

FLOATING WORLD

THE BRITISH MUSEUM

FLOATING WORLD

JAPAN IN THE EDO PERIOD

John Reeve

THE BRITISH MUSEUM PRESS

Thanks to Mavis Pilbeam of the Japanese section in the
Department of Asia, Nina Shandloff and Beatriz Waters of BM Press,
designer Peter Ward, and BM photographers Jerome Perkins,
John Williams and Kevin Lovelock.

Frontispiece: Detail from Parody of Narihira's Journey to the East,
1797–8, by Kitigawa Utamaro (1753–1806).
The complete triptych is reproduced on pp. 38–9.

© 2006 The Trustees of the British Museum
First published in 2006 by The British Museum Press
A division of The British Museum Company Ltd
38 Russell Square, London WC1B 3QQ
www.britishmuseum.co.uk

John Reeve has asserted his moral right to be identified
as the author of this work

A catalogue record for this book is available from the British Library

ISBN-13:   978-0-7141-2434-6
ISBN-10:   0-7141-2434-6

Photography by British Museum Department of Photography and Imaging
Designed and typeset in Centaur by Peter Ward
Printed in China by C&C Offset Printing Co., Ltd

THE BRITISH MUSEUM
WITHDRAWN
THE PAUL HAMLYN LIBRARY

769.952
REE

Japanese Pictures
of the Floating World

Living only for the moment, turning our full attention to the pleasures of the moon, sun, the cherry blossoms and the maple leaves, singing songs, drinking wine, and diverting ourselves just in floating, floating, caring not a whit for the pauperism staring us in the face, refusing to be disheartened, like a gourd floating along with the river current: this is what we call the floating world, 'ukiyo'.

Asai Ryoi, *Tales of the Floating World* (*c.* 1661), trans. Richard Lane

This is how one seventeenth-century Japanese writer described what was becoming a remarkable phenomenon in his time. By 1700 the population of Edo (modern Tokyo) had reached a million, making it one of the largest cities in the world. This sudden transformation – from a swampy village to a bustling metropolis in just a century – was like the rapid emergence of new American cities in the nineteenth century.

'Ukiyo' was a state of mind as well as a world of pleasure seeking. Within a highly regulated society, it promised a release from the restraints imposed by the government and samurai warrior class on the merchant class and urban life generally. Not surprisingly, the pleasure districts of Edo, Kyoto and Osaka were also regulated. The most famous of these was the Yoshiwara, a separate walled town to the north of the main city, entirely designed to amuse its male population. This book illuminates a self-contained world of pleasure and sensation as experienced by male connoisseurs of beautiful women, sex, ravishing landscapes, raunchy theatre and serenity of the spirit. It begins behind the scenes, with the household maids at dawn. The comfort and pleasure world of Edo for men and its wealthier women inhabitants was made possible by the efforts of large numbers of women in the service industries, idolized and idealized by male artists for the male gaze: 'a world of men obsessed with women'. Ukiyo-e paintings and prints also reflect the artists' fascination with depicting life at all levels of society. In this respect they are not unlike Hogarth, Gillray, Rowlandson or Goya, their contemporaries in Europe, who also wanted to show life as it was, and to satirize the rich and powerful.

During the Edo period the Japanese were forbidden to travel or to build ocean-going ships, but they were not entirely cut off from the outside world, and some took a keen interest in the inventions and peculiarities of foreigners. The first Europeans to arrive were the Portuguese in 1542, bringing Christianity, muskets and tobacco. Known as Namban, 'southern barbarians', they were fascinating for their strange hats, long legs and breeches. The activities of the Jesuit missionaries in particular led to trouble, and in 1639 the shogun banned all foreigners, except the Dutch and Chinese, who were restricted to Nagasaki in the far southwest of Japan. This remained the case until the arrival of the American Commodore Perry and his 'black-dragon ships' in 1853.

Japanese prints had an especially strong impact on the Impressionists and other nineteenth-century Western artists. The French composer Claude Debussy chose a version of Hokusai's 'The Great Wave' (p. 16) for the cover of his score for 'La Mer'; Edouard Manet owned a copy of it. Van Gogh copied it, as did Hiroshige and others: he also collected over 400 Japanese prints, many of which are now in the Van Gogh Museum in Amsterdam. 'Even the most vulgar Japanese sheets [of woodblock prints] coloured in flat tones are as admirable as Rubens and Veronese', he wrote. The novelist Emile Zola, portrayed by Manet with a Japanese screen in the background (1868, Louvre, Paris), was another enthusiast for Japanese prints and 'their strange elegance and splendid colour patches'. Toulouse-Lautrec lived in the red light district of Paris and knew its inhabitants as intimately as some Ukiyo-e artists knew the Yoshiwara area of Edo. He was inspired by Japanese prints, calligraphy and decorative arts in his work, notably a poster for Le Divan Japonais, a Paris nightclub (1893).

The British Museum has one of the world's outstanding collections of Japanese arts from this period, through which we can catch a special glimpse of a vanished world, still fresh and visually rewarding to even the most jaded modern eye. This book evokes a day in the life of Edo Japan. Beginning at dawn, we see people at work and leisure: servants and artists, actors and audiences, courtesans and customers. Exploring the pleasure districts of old Edo, we visit the kabuki theatre and a sūmo match. We can admire the work of kimono designers, screen painters and lacquer craftsmen on display in luxury stores. We observe beautiful women on the street, and in upper rooms and brothels: beauties of the teahouses and sophisticated courtesans as well as prostitutes (some past their best). We can also escape the heat and bustle of the city to experience nature, sea and landscape, from that famous Great Wave to Mount Fuji in all its splendour. As the Edo era ends with the arrival of foreigners, after centuries of relative seclusion, we can look at ourselves through Japanese eyes and also understand why Western artists were so excited by their discovery of this quintessentially Japanese art. Evening is a time for intimacy but also allows us to pause and reflect at a mountain shrine as the evening bell tolls. Finally, as the rays of the rising sun turn Fuji red, another day begins.

The dawn of day –
On the tip of the barley leaf
The frost of spring

UEJIMA ONITSURA (1661–1738)

Early morning was less poetic for servants:

Now that dawn has come
Perhaps the foxes will eat
Those cursed roosters,
Crowing in the early morn . . .

TAKIZAWA BAKIN, *The Biographies of Eight Dogs* (1814–41)

THE COCKS have already crowed, the temple bells have rung, and soon it will be time for these servants to cough politely outside the doors of their master and mistress. These maids are only just awake, and slightly dishevelled as they fix their hair at the well: fires have to be lit and water boiled for the morning tea and baths. Some mistresses were especially demanding of their servants: the one caricatured by novelist Ejima Kiseki in his *Characters of Worldly Young Women* (1716) decides to admire morning glories in the cool of early morning:

And so that night she leaves orders to fill tiers of lacquer boxes with savoury rice, prepared exactly to her taste . . . 'Have the bath ready before six. As to my hair, you may do it in three folds . . . It must all seem quite perfect: you know how the neighbours stare.'

Drawing water for breakfast, coloured woodblock print,
1795–1800, by Kitigawa Utamaro (1753–1806).

Utamaro, like Hokusai and several other artists featured in this book, has a recognizable artistic personality. He was not only an admirer of female beauty and grace, and a skilled creator of atmosphere and understatement, as seen in some of his erotic prints. He also exquisitely captured the essence of shells, birds and insects. One of his teachers praised his 'painting from the heart'. This image is from an illustrated book, evidence of the explosion of publishing in Edo Japan in which coloured woodblock printing played a crucial role in making books of this calibre available to a wider public.

In this scene the tables are turned so that the models are looking at the artist as he decorates a room in a 'Green House', a high-class bordello. These gorgeously dressed ladies are courtesans who, in entertaining their wealthy clients, were not only expected to talk knowledgeably about art and poetry, music and cuisine, but also to sing and write poetry. The setting was also often luxurious, in the spirit of 'kazari' – a delight in sumptuous decoration that extended to sedan chairs, lacquer objects and painted screens.

In their rich and brightly coloured plumage, they too are like rare birds. The phoenix, red bird of the south, was a symbol both of summer and of the empress in Chinese art, a major source of inspiration for all aspects of Japanese culture and religion, painting and sculpture, literature and design. The phoenix is also an emblem of rebirth – appropriate for a combustible, largely wooden city that regularly suffered fires and was therefore constantly being rebuilt, even in more recent times.

The artist painting a phoenix, diptych of colour
woodblock prints, published in 'Picture Book of
Events of the Year in the Green Houses', 1804,
by Kitagawa Utamaro (1753–1806).

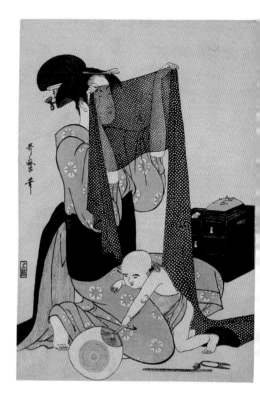

Women sewing, triptych of colour
woodblock prints, *c.* 1795–6,
by Kitagawa Utamaro (1753–1806).

THERE WERE good reasons for rising early, especially on a humid summer day, when even the lightest of clothes stick to the skin. Utamaro brilliantly conveys all this with the lightest of touches: one or two strands of hair out of place give the merest suggestion of dishevelment. These respectable ladies are handling thin gauzy material, innately sensuous. They are folding and mending sashes and also peeking through gauze – evidence of technical skill in printmaking that we are meant to notice. The gorgeous clothes worn in illustrations

throughout this book required a great deal of maintenance and attention and were an immediate expression of identity within a precisely calibrated visual language.

This triptych shows a consummate Japanese artist orchestrating a sense of space and movement flowing across three panels, with two parallel groups and skilful positioning of objects such as the kettle. While one lady looks at pet insects in their cage, a boy taunts a cat with its image in a mirror, and a baby plays with a fan.

HOKUSAI'S REPUTATION was made in the West by these highly original and inventive picture books, manga, which resemble a cartoonist's sketchbook. Altogether he created nearly 4000 such images, in 15 volumes – an astonishing and highly original achievement that was not only influential in Japan. It is said the French artist Felix Bracquemond (1833–1914) first came upon Japanese prints like these in Paris in 1856, while unwrapping imported Japanese ceramics and lacquer wares, for which rejected proofs of Hokusai's manga had been used as wrapping paper. He showed them to fellow artists – and Japonisme was born. In modern Japan manga are rather different illustrated picture books, catering for all tastes, and modern manga, like Hokusai's, have devotees all over the world.

Humour is never far away in Hokusai's work. Here he is lampooning the samurai class of warriors, who had become divorced from their original fighting role, like knights in England during the same period. Samurai, whether involved in government or not, were required to spend much of the year in Edo rather than on their estates in the countryside. Like Louis XIV and the French aristocracy, the shoguns who ruled Japan emasculated the regional standing and potential power bases of the daimyo, the leading samurai, and ensured their wealth was spent on consumption rather than warfare. Urban life in Edo revolved around them. Minor samurai, like those depicted here, lost their status and often ended up as poor hangers-on – a theme taken up by modern film makers.

Warriors at ease, colour woodblock print,
published in 'Ten Thousand Sketches'
by Katsushika Hokusai (1760–1849).

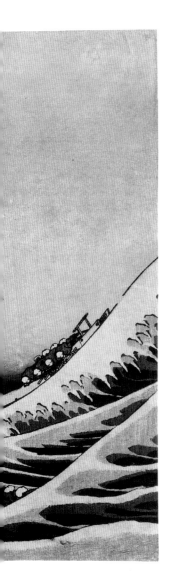

Viewed from a moving boat, even mountains
    move —
But do the mountain pines know this? ...
A wave is but a single thing, we're told; but from
    its hue
You'd think it was a mixture — flowers and snow!

The Tosa Diary (*c.* 936)

THIS IMAGE of Fuji has become so familiar it is almost impossible to see it afresh. Prussian blue pigment from China had just become cheaply available and was much longer lasting than the blue used in earlier prints, in which the colour has since faded. Thousands of impressions of this print were made from the original block, and countless more from new ones. Hokusai expresses succinctly the relation of mountain and sea and the perils of both, beyond human control.

This print is meant to be read from right to left, so that the wave threatens to engulf the viewer, too. The waves are claw-like, as if animated and reaching out to grasp the fragile boat, which has a protective Shintō torii arch on its bow.

Under the wave, off Kanagawa (southwest
of Tokyo), colour woodblock print, 1829–33,
by Katsushika Hokusai (1760–1849).

HOKUSAI HERE CREATES a sense of depth around two triangles, separated by mist and cloud, for an abstract and dreamlike effect, showing man pitted against the elements. Above the churning waters where two mountain streams flow violently into each other, a fisherman perches precariously on what looks like a piece of stage scenery. At the ends of his lines are cormorants, used for fishing as in ancient China. To his left a young boy huddles with a basket for the catch. The poet Yosa Buson (1716–83) noted the 'dreadful intensity' of the angler.

Meat was forbidden under strict Buddhism, and an early European traveller observed of the Japanese that 'fish, rootes and rice are their common junkets . . . they have the same kyndes of beastes that we have, but they seldom eat anye fleshe . . .' This print exists in many different colour combinations, some entirely in shades of blue, others with violet, green, pink and red touches.

A fisherman at Kajikazawa, colour woodblock print, *c.* 1831, by Katsushika Hokusai (1760–1849).

Imaginary scene of women
producing woodblock prints, triptych
of colour woodblock prints, 1857,
by Utagawa Kunisada (1786–1864).

HERE WOMEN ARE imagined doing men's work: they are cutting through the drawing on to the block (right panel), then cutting the block and preparing the paper (centre). The colours (left panel) were not mixed to produce shades, as in Western art, but used as uniform blocks, strengthened or darkened by adjusting the amount of water or white pigment. The same sheet of paper had to be placed carefully on to each separate colour block, often between ten and twenty in number. Great skill was needed to make sure that all these colour blocks were precisely aligned to print without blurred outlines or overlaps.

Prints were made on single sheets or two, three or even six sheets, and 200 impressions might be made for one edition – a week's work for a printer. Works by popular artists such as Hokusai or Hiroshige might require as many as 10,000 impressions, at a time when a colour print cost the same as a bowl of noodles. Some artists were extraordinarily productive; Kunisada produced over 50,000 designs, whereas a prolific Western artist of the same era, such as Daumier, might manage up to 8000.

食事之間管絃之贈

THIS SECTION of the handscroll shows the Dutch on the man-made island of Deshima, off Nagasaki, where they were confined by the shoguns. It is probably an eighteenth-century copy of a painting from *c.* 1700 by Watanabe Shūseki (1637–1707) for the shogun in Edo. The Dutch are depicted in an upper room of their harbour-front building (a ship's mast can be seen at front right, flying the Dutch flag), dining at a high table – a strange custom from the Japanese perspective. Next

door they and their Japanese guest listen to music, played on European instruments, possibly by Indonesian servants (brought from the Asian headquarters of the Dutch empire). The edible livestock outside reflect the Japanese amazement at how much meat these foreigners ate.

The Dutch and Chinese settlements at Nagasaki,
detail from a pair of handscroll paintings, 18th century.

23

T HE MAIN WATERWAY of Edo, the Sumida River, ran through the low-lying commercial district in the eastern part of the city. By the mid-eighteenth century, Edo had grown into an enormous city of over a million inhabitants, with its own distinctive culture. People began to take pride in the river, seeing it as a suitable subject for artists. These scrolls are among the earliest detailed depictions of the Sumida River, showing it through the seasons. This scene is Ryōgoku Bridge, built after a disastrous fire in the 1650s with large plazas as firebreaks at either end, which attracted street performers, side shows and firework displays. The bridge is shown partly from below to display the wonders of its

construction. Hiroshige also depicted bridges in this way, inspiring the American artist Whistler to do likewise for the Thames in London. In this painting, people crossing the bridge are carefully described, but the topography and other detail are hazy so as not to distract from the bridge itself and the impression of a teeming metropolis on the move.

Scenes along the length of the Sumida River,
detail from a set of three handscroll paintings,
c. 1751–71, by Kanō Kyūei.

A new coloured print for the opening of the season, triptych of colour woodblock prints, *c.* 1795, by Katsukawa Shun'ei (1762–1819).

IN THE CENTRE PANEL of this triptych can be glimpsed the inside of a kabuki theatre and its long walkway (hanamichi). In the right panel, three ladies arrive at the theatre with their lunch carried by a servant behind them, as some performances lasted all day. On the left, a family is being persuaded to buy something, and teashop girls await customers. Like this print, kabuki plays depicted scenes from everyday life in Edo as well as historical and heroic subjects — not unlike Shakespeare.

One finds a tavern at every five paces; and it is as if this city had
been changed into a pond of rice-wine . . . If there is a rattling like
peals of thunder, it is the ox-carts on the side streets. Ladies with
girdles of spun gold sway their hips; and their garments . . . flow as
do the torrents of spring. The black and white prints of earlier
days are antiquated now, and the only thing people care for is the
newly devised gorgeousness of the[se] Pictures.

'An Account of Dohei the sweetmeat seller', 1769

Inside a kabuki theatre, triptych
of colour woodblock prints by
Utagawa Toyokuni I (1769–1825).

KABUKI THEATRE (literally 'frolicking') expresses perfectly the spirited
combination of raucous humour, colourful drama and poetry that
strongly appealed to the urban citizens of Edo, Osaka and Kyoto, each
of which had their own distinctive styles. Governments frequently
attempted to regulate or close it down, for not only did kabuki have
dangerous potential for satire and comment, it also attracted loose
sexual behaviour: female actors were banned in 1629, and later the boys
who had taken over their roles.

This triptych shows how close the audience were to the actors: eating, drinking, quarrelling and calling out their names. As in Shakespearean theatres, there is a small timber house on the main stage, with a curtain pulled across before the performance begins. Often a large revolve stage and lifts enabled sudden changes and surprise entries; other quick costume changes might take place on stage, to great applause. At left is the hanamichi, the walkway enabling a star actor to make a dramatic entrance through the audience, to a rapturous response.

Actors as the lovers Umegawa and Chubei,
colour woodblock print, 1794, by Tōshūsai Sharaku.

Kabuki fans had an insatiable demand for images of their favourite actors. Sharaku is famous for his actor prints, although he appears to have worked only for ten months in 1794–5, and the results as here are memorable. Certain actors specialized in the women's roles (onnagata), as Ganjuro III so brilliantly does today. It seems extraordinary how convincingly middle-aged men could impersonate young women while still obviously being men. Onnagata, like leading courtesans, set the women's fashions of the day.

Overleaf (left): The actor Otani Oniji, colour
woodblock print, 1794, by Tōshūsai Sharaku.

Overleaf (right): The actor Ichikawa Ebizō,
colour woodblock print, 1796,
by Utagawa Kunimasa (1773–1810).

Overleaf two kabuki actors glare at each other. Otani Oniji (*left*) is characterized by Sharaku as a bad guy. Kunimasa's print of Ichikawa Ebizō (*right*) is a tribute to a great actor on his retirement in 1796, zooming in on the climax of one of his most celebrated roles. It is a masterpiece of compressed energy. He is shown in the shibaraku scene, when, with a thundering cry of 'Shibaraku!' ('Wait a moment!'), the hero bursts on to the hanamichi walkway from the back of the theatre, just in time to save the characters on stage from certain death. Ebizō wears a characteristic scowl and red make-up, and on his costume are the three interlocking white squares that make up the Ichikawa family emblem.

M ANY OF TODAY'S kabuki stars are descended from long family
pedigrees. One of the most famous is that of this actor: Ichikawa
Danjūrō VII. Here Kunisada convincingly shows him crazed, at the
moment in the play when he conjures up a storm on a mountain.
Branches of blossom, like fans, hats and swords, are important props and
signifiers in kabuki. Kunisada, in his set of prints capturing actors in
their star roles, revives the use of mica backgrounds and is staking his
claim to be the heir of Sharaku. The result can be rather dark now, as
here, but still forceful, and looks forward to the prints of the Meiji
restoration. Kunisada was one of the most prolific of all Ukiyo-e print
designers, with 20,000 designs in total, so they are not all masterpieces.

Danjūrō VII (1791–1859), a poet and artist himself, was one of the
most remarkable of all kabuki actors. His family emblem can also be
seen on a fan (p. 27, right-hand panel) and a costume (p. 33); Danjūrō
VIII also figures (p. 36).

Kan Shojo, colour woodblock print, 1815,
by Utagawa Kunisada (1786–1864).

THE OCCASION for this print is two-fold: the boys' festival, and the departure of the celebrated kabuki actor, Ichikawa Danjūrō VIII, to visit his exiled father (seen in the previous print). Evil spirits are believed to be at their worst on the fifth day of the fifth month, so any family with a boy under the age of seven would hang a paper or cloth carp banner from their roof. Carp, especially when swimming upstream, represent perseverance in Japanese art (p. 61). This print was commissioned by a poetry club of fishmongers – the actor's logo was also a lobster.

This is an example of surimono, literally 'printed things,' which were privately printed and distributed, usually for special occasions. The actor's father is here shown in a famous role as Shōki the demon-queller on one banner, pursuing the demon on the other banner which flutters to the left – a delightful and ingenious touch. Retirements from the stage were celebrated in suitably theatrical fashion: actors on Osaka kabuki prints were depicted flying away on a crane like a Chinese Immortal, or going to Nirvana like the Buddha.

A farewell surimono for Ichikawa Danjūrō VIII, colour
woodblock print, 1849, by Utagawa Kuniyoshi (1797–1861).

Parody of Narihira's Journey to the East, triptych of colour woodblock prints, 1797–8, by Kitagawa Utamaro (1753–1806).

THIS IS ANOTHER kind of cross-dressing. It is possible that this print records one of the costume parades performed each autumn in the Yoshiwara pleasure quarter as part of the Niwaka Festival. Male and female geisha in fanciful costumes would process around the quarter on floats or with other elaborate props. Female geisha would sometimes dress as men for these events. The hairstyles of the figures here are clearly feminine, though each either wears or carries some kind of man's court headgear.

This is also probably a 'parody picture', which reworks an episode from the Tales of Ise entitled 'Journey to the East'. The upper figures on

the centre and right-hand sheets impersonate the author of most of the tales, the ninth-century courtier-poet Ariwara no Narihira, and a standard-bearing retainer. When Narihira thought he was going to die he wrote these lines:

> That it is a road
> Which some day we all travel
> I had heard before,
> Yet I never expected
> To take it so soon myself

The pre-match procession at a sumō tournament, triptych of colour woodblock prints, 1796, by Katsukawa Shun'ei (1762–1819).

SUMŌ WRESTLERS are enormous, but not quite as colossal as this. Shun'ei has shown them here parading in their characteristic tasselled aprons, under a canopy that resembles a Shintō shrine: sumō originated as part of the Shintō religion, perhaps 2000 years ago. Sumō tournaments were held at shrines as part of harvest thanksgivings, and even today the referee is dressed as a Shintō priest. Sumō became a professionalized spectator sport during the Edo period and is now watched by millions on television, and not just in Japan.

The audience here appears to be entirely male, though women were also fans: two of novelist Ejima Kiseki's bored 'modern matrons' suddenly perk up at news of a wrestling match: ' "Shichigoro takes on the Thunderbolt!" they cry. "We can't miss it!" Off they dash, in sedan chairs decorated by autumn landscapes or sprinkled gold.' Such fans also had an insatiable demand for images of their favourite wrestlers, like that for kabuki actors and famous beauties.

THE TEASHOP was one of the many venues for male pleasure in the densely populated urban world of Edo. Ohisa was the daughter of the proprietor of the Takashima chain of cake and teashops in Edo and seems to have made her reputation serving tea at the family shop near Ryōgoku Bridge (pp. 24–5). She was a favourite subject of several Ukiyo-e print artists in the 1790s, especially Kitagawa Utamaro. Here Ohisa's black gauze kimono bears a pattern of yellow and white flashes, and the design on her sash is of a plover wheeling above stylized waves. Her fan bears her family's triple oak-leaf crest.

On this print her beauty is celebrated in a poem (top left) by Karabana Tadaaya:

> Charms and tea are brimming over
> And neither gets cold!
> Let me not wake
> From this lucky dream of the New Year
> At Takashimaya.

Utamaro was the master of this type of half-length portrait, capturing the essence of female beauty and particularly the back of the neck, a key erogenous zone. The freshness and grace of this kind of woodblock print were to have a profound influence on French and other Western artists later in the century. Japanese prints became easily available after the Meiji restoration opened Japan to the outside world, and Japanese art could be seen at world fairs and exhibitions.

Ohisa of the Takashimaya teashop, colour woodblock print, c. 1792–3, by Kitagawa Utamaro (1753–1806).

THE FOUR SEASONS restaurant was very popular, famous for its highly original fish cuisine, and attracted varied ranks of society. In the restaurant garden, flowers of the four seasons were supposedly in bloom all year round. On the reed matting we can see a geisha tuning up her stringed shamisen, while two others play the fox game. Tea is being served, and raw fish are brought in on a tray. Outside there are lanterns, boats on the Sumida River (perhaps bringing more customers?) and a distant view of the city, including a watchtower for fires — essential with such combustible wooden buildings.

Shumman was a poet as well as a prolific painter. He specialized in showing elegantly dressed women, and used vivid colours which are not necessarily meant to reflect accurately the colours of the real world. They are still vivid today, except for the blue of the river. Only from about 1830 did printmakers have access to a blue that did not fade: Hokusai's Great Wave dates from that year and demonstrates this new colour (p. 16).

All the elements of this composition are framed in an unusual way and cropped as if glimpsed from elsewhere in the restaurant, or from the outside. The composition is built on strong diagonals: low fences, the riverside, rows of warehouses and other buildings on the other side. The diagonals give the space great energy: Japanese prints are seldom static. To help create this effect, the artist has eliminated the sliding screens from the corner and side of the room facing the river, so we can see how it opens directly on to a verandah extending all the way around the building.

A party in the Four Seasons restaurant by the Sumida River, diptych of colour woodblock prints, c. 1786, by Kubo Shumman (1757–1820).

THERE WAS great public interest in what went on backstage at the theatre. Everyone here is male, including trainee female imperson- ators (onnagata), who also sometimes worked as homosexual prostitutes and might meet their rich patrons in teahouses such as this. At the centre right a blind masseur soothes the shoulders of a client, while one actor serves him sake and another plays the stringed shamisen. Another actor can be glimpsed with his wealthy samurai client through a mosquito net in a bedroom. The furnishings include tatami mats, scroll

paintings (displayed in the alcove at the back), a sliding fusuma door decorated with a scene of snowy pines, and lacquered furniture. Moronobu was a great early pioneer of Ukiyo-e from the 1670s and produced more than a hundred illustrated books and many erotic album prints.

Scenes in a theatre teahouse, handscroll painting, 1685,
by Hishikawa Moronobu (d. 1694).

47

A pleasure boat on the Sumida River,
triptych of colour woodblock prints,
c. 1785–8, by Torii Kiyonaga (1752–1815).

TORII KIYONAGA was one of the most accomplished of Ukiyo-e artists, and eventually headed the Torii school of artists. He painted scenes of everyday Japanese life as well as designing erotic and kabuki prints. His more naturalistic style in the 1770s influenced Utamaro among others, and in the 1780s he featured beautiful women in full-

length portraits, bijin-ga (prints of beauties). He is especially adept at grouping figures, as here. Pleasure-boat parties are a lyrical genre in Ukiyo-e art. This scene, as in Shumman's restaurant (p. 45), is of a group of sophisticated Edo people, unlike the Osaka boat party that follows on the next page, which shows a different clientele altogether.

OSAKA WAS 'the rice-bowl of Japan', and like Kyoto had a population of 400,000. Osaka also had a pleasure quarter similar to that of Edo, which catered (like its kabuki) almost entirely for the tastes of merchants. As one historian has observed, 'only in the brothel and theatre district could merchants rise to a social position that was equivalent to their wealth'. Osaka also had its own distinctive artists, such as Ichiami Sōkyū and Saitō Shūho (who were actually the same person). Here and in the next illustration (p. 53) he is lively and crisp, though he later became a more humdrum Kanō School artist.

This picaresque tour through the wonders of the Shinmachi pleasure district takes in street singers, geisha, workmen, courtesans and customers. Shūho also depicted life in Kyoto, boosting the self-image of both traditional rivals to Edo, while at the same time displaying their rough edges. Osaka prints from the 1790s can seem more awkward than those from Edo, and even more focused on the strange and the supernatural. Other early nineteenth-century Osaka artists include Hirosada, Shunchō and Ryūsai.

Evening river party, colour woodblock print published
in the album 'Mr Aoi's Chronicle of Charm', 1803,
by Ichiami Sōkyū (1769–1859).

THIS IS THE OPENING page of a three-volume tribute to the vibrant life of Osaka, and appropriately it is New Year. The procession makes a strong diagonal across the page; like the book itself, it would be read from right to left. The clients of these courtesans were merchants, and not surprisingly they wanted to see their own world of conspicuous consumption depicted in art, just as much as courtiers, samurai or devout Buddhists wanted their own particular worlds reflected. Depicted here is the New Year display of kimonos, gifts from wealthy clients. The number and expense of your new kimonos showed how popular and desirable you were. Such processions could be big events, with the staff of the pleasure houses joining in. This one is on its way to the Buddhist temple of Aizen Myo-O, with maids and child attendants. Their umbrellas display the aptly phallic logo of their brothel – a mallet!

Cecila Segawa Seigle has pointed out that 'the courtesan in procession was not a normal human being: she was a figure on the stage . . . and had to maintain her composure throughout. She ignored all acquaintances, friends, and lovers. Addressed, she did not respond and kept her eyes straight ahead. At most she might smile slightly or nod.'

The strong diagonal from bottom right to top left is a feature of prints like these, whether they are flocks of birds or blossoms on branches. This idea appealed to the French Impressionists and can be seen, for example, in Toulouse-Lautrec's print, 'Le jockey'.

Courtesans on parade, colour woodblock print published
in the album 'Mr Aoi's Chronicle of Charm', 1803,
by Saitō Shūho (1769–1859).

JAPANESE ARTISTS knew about perspective in Western art and manipulated it for their own purposes: ironically it was dramatic foreshortening, as in this print, that appealed so much to Western artists such as Manet and Toulouse-Lautrec, a century or more later. This scene in an Edo brothel is certainly theatrical in its staging, like a coy peep show in a box. There is a mood of expectation, not surprisingly, and a few hints that events are heating up (on the left and in the distant right). Otherwise the customers are just relaxing, smoking, playing a board game and listening to music. Like the painting of the theatre teahouse (pp. 46–7), it gives an excellent idea of how traditional Japanese buildings were constructed.

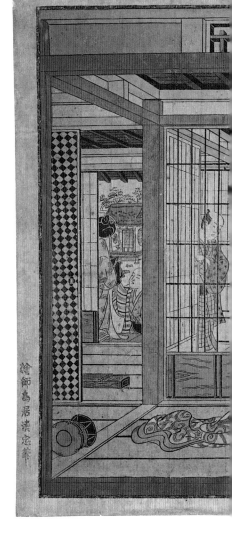

The Daimonjiya brothel,
colour woodblock print, 1745–50,
by Torii Kiyotada.

新吉原仲ノ町　大文字屋座敷

通油町

奥村源政画

55

THE YOSHIWARA pleasure quarter, on the northern edge of the city of Edo, was the only area licensed for prostitution. As many as 3000 women worked there, from lowly streetwalkers to exclusive high-ranking courtesans. This was truly the 'floating world' of fleeting pleasures, where distinctions between classes could be blurred and government regulations suspended. Kitao Masanobu, who also wrote novels, established himself as chief guide and arbiter in the exclusive world of the high-ranking courtesans of the Yoshiwara. Many other artists, including Harunobu, Shigemasa and Kiyonaga, competed in producing tributes to them in colour woodblock prints, illustrated books and albums.

This sumptuous image comes from an album, designed by Masanobu and compiled by the ambitious and energetic publisher Tsutaya Jūsaburō in an attempt to surpass all competitors. The large format is twice the size of normal single-sheet prints, and the colour printing is of outstanding complexity and richness. Poetry was all the rage in Edo Japan, and each print also includes waka poems, reproducing the actual handwriting of the women depicted.

Waka are classically 31-syllable verses: haiku (17-syllable verses) were originally the opening part of a waka sequence, but later developed independently following the simpler style of Matsuo Bashō (1644–94).

The literary courtesans Hinazuru and Chōzan, colour woodblock print
published in the album 'The contest of New Yoshiwara courtesans with
examples of their calligraphy', 1784, by Kitao Masanobu (1761–1816).

Courtesans of the Tamaya House,
six-fold screen painting, late 1770s
or early 1780s, attributed to
Utagawa Toyoharu (1735–1814).

THIS IS ONE of the most important surviving Ukiyo-e paintings of its
period (recently restored). A group of high-ranking courtesans are
seated on the red carpet in the centre, surrounded by their apprentices, in
pairs with matching kimonos around the walls. This is the latticed display
room of a brothel in the Yoshiwara pleasure quarter, where the women sit
waiting for clients. It appears to be the quiet middle period of the day, and
the courtesans are amusing themselves in various ways – smoking, playing

the shamisen and dressing a doll. One of the teenage apprentices has
dozed off. Among the lacquered accessories depicted in the front, to the
right of the smoking set, is a small box decorated with the emblem of a
flying crane. According to a printed guide to courtesans published in 1788,
this was a crest used by Komurasaki, a high-ranking courtesan in the house
run by Tamaya Sansaburō. The name of the house appears on the entrance
curtain towards the centre back.

THIS EXTRAVAGANTLY elaborate kimono, probably a New Year gift from a wealthy client, is obviously bulky and imprisons its wearer as though she were a kind of sculpture. Her profusion of tortoiseshell hairpins are carved with flowers at their tips. Her sash or obi, with its striking pattern of crosses, is tied in an enormous knot at the front, and she holds one end of its scarlet lining behind her head to show off the radiating hairpins. She is turning so as to display the fabulous design of swimming carp, which was probably painted directly on to the silk. The carp is a symbol of perseverance, perhaps appropriately for her profession. The image of a carp climbing a waterfall, found in prints by Gakutei among many others, recalls the Chinese legend of a carp crossing rapids and turning into a dragon. Carp banners are flown from roofs during the annual boys' festival (p. 36).

Although Gakutei was a native of Edo, he lived and worked in Osaka in the 1830s. His work was much influenced by Hokusai, yet he is distinctive and original. He was also a poet and put his own poems on his prints. Popular in his time, he was an extremely accomplished craftsman who made many excellent surimono and book illustrations.

Courtesan wearing a kimono decorated with swimming carp, hanging scroll painting, 1818–30, by Yashima Gakutei (1786–1868).

THE FORMAT of a hanging scroll offers erotic potential in the slow unrolling of an image such as this. Such scrolls would be selected for viewing on special occasions but were not meant to be on permanent display.

This courtesan is shown with her normally white face flushed and her hair slightly astray. She turns to look at her client and reveals her neck, a key erogenous zone, to the viewer. She has already removed her vivid scarlet crepe silk sash (obi), and is drawing her arm from her right sleeve. In her left hand she holds a headrest and pillow, in readiness. Her angular features are characteristic of portraits by artists such as Yoshitoshi's teacher, Kuniyoshi. She is not a conventional beauty in the Utamaro mould and is past her prime. Yoshitoshi eventually married a former geisha, and he shows great sympathy in depicting such women. The visual tension, as in Op Art, between the diamond weave of the sleeping mat and the fine blue dots of her tie-dyed kimono also contributes to a sense of agitation and sensuality.

Tsukioka Yoshitoshi has been called the last genius of Ukiyo-e. He lived through the dramatic upheavals of the Meiji period and, although strongly influenced by Western art, worked with traditional Japanese subject matter.

Courtesan undressing, hanging scroll painting, 1865–70,
by Tsukioka Yoshitoshi (1839–92).

Notes on women's conduct: stretching fabrics, triptych of colour woodblock prints, 1842, by Utagawa Kuniyoshi (1797–1861).

SERVANTS ARE HERE washing a sash (obi) and hanging it out to dry. The maids are wearing wooden pattens (geta) to keep their own improbably elegant kimonos out of the water and dirt – it is a fashion plate rather than a piece of social reportage. Not only is this a tour de force of animated and flowing design, but also of printmaking, given the number of colours involved. Van Gogh was among Kuniyoshi's many admirers and collected his work.

Kuniyoshi (Yoshitoshi's master) created a series of images of virtuous

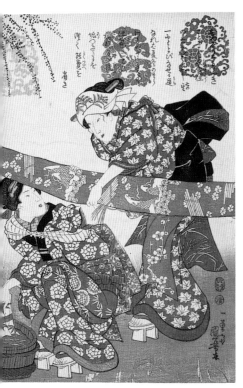

women at work as a way of evading the harsh censorship laws of the 1840s, which banned the images of courtesans, beautiful women and kabuki actors in which Kuniyoshi had specialized, like his master Toyokuni. Kuniyoshi also created prints of ghost stories and of warriors and legends, but these also landed him in trouble when he satirized the shogun. The woodblock of the offending design and remaining stocks of unsold prints were destroyed, and Kuniyoshi was reprimanded.

PEOPLE IN EDO JAPAN were fascinated with images not only of
themselves, of beauties, actors, ghosts and urban life, but also of the
natural world. Artists such as Utamaro, Hokusai, Hiroshige and
Masayoshi obliged with exquisite illustrated books. Cockles, clams and
crabs were illustrated with haiku to show the 'Boon of the Seas' (Ryusui,
1762). Elsewhere cats pounce on birds and falcons on monkeys, frogs
gather by the stream, and armies of insects march along.

Kitao Masayoshi was commissioned to copy an earlier Chinese artist's
paintings of birds imported to Nagasaki from China in 1762, including
these partridges. They were published in a deluxe woodblock-printed
album at the end of 1790. The partridges are outlined in black, in the usual
Ukiyo-e style. The landscape behind is an attempt to simulate the rather
dreamy and stylized conventions of Chinese landscape painting, which had
such a profound influence on Japanese art. Masayoshi is noted for his
sketchbooks and for his caricatured 'simplified forms of drawing birds
and animals', but also for consummate paintings of birds such as owls
and falcons and for prints and paintings of flowers, as well as the usual
beauties and ghost scenes.

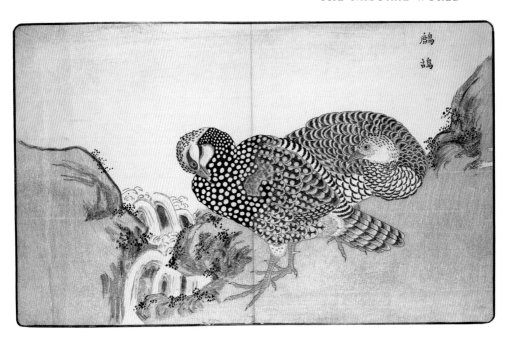

鷓
鴣

Partridges, colour woodblock print published in an album entitled
'Pictures of Imported Birds', 1790, by Kitao Masayoshi (1764–1824).

THE QUALITY of these paintings and their use of gold leaf indicate a rich patron. Whereas in traditional panoramas we peer through gold clouds at tantalizing details of a city, festival or battle, in this case we can follow each scene as the scrolls are unrolled. Here early eighteenth-century citizens of Edo are enjoying the cherry blossom in spring, an opportunity for picnics, music and a peep show (a new Western import, for which many artists supplied images). The Kan'eji Temple (rebuilt after one of Edo's most disastrous fires) is on the right, with worshippers including samurai, with their two swords, alongside people of other classes.

Viewing cherry blossom is a ritual that continues to this day, as a way of marking the seasons. The passing of spring is a common feature of Japanese poetry:

> Spring soon ends –
> Birds will weep while in
> The eyes of fish are tears.

MATSUO BASHŌ (1644–94)

Views of Ueno and Asakusa,
detail from a pair of handscroll paintings, 1716–36.

69

Asukayama at cherry blossom time, triptych of colour woodblock prints, c. 1785, by Torii Kiyonaga (1752–1815).

THIS HAS BEEN hailed as a landmark in the development of Ukiyo-e printmaking: for the first time, European pictorial conventions have been thoroughly and effortlessly integrated into a Japanese print. It is also unusual in its mix of social classes: on the left the young daughter of a feudal lord (daimyo) is led by her nurses, while on the right are

ordinary shopgirls. A telescope is being used in the background of the centre print. Asukayama was a celebrated beauty spot, preserved for viewing cherry blossom at the end of March (like Ueno in the previous painting). In this triptych (like the next one) Kiyonaga arranges his figures lyrically, setting them against the fresh colours of spring.

Women visiting Enoshima,
triptych of colour woodblock prints,
c. 1785–8, by Torii Kiyonaga (1752–1815).

THIS BEAUTIFULLY staged triptych is a reminder of the world of
mountain and sea that so fascinated Edo artists. Hokusai famously
depicted Mount Fuji in all its moods and colours and here it can be seen
from Katase Beach. A collection of elegantly dressed pilgrim travellers
from the city wait at a tea stall for low tide, when they will be able
to cross the causeway to the sacred island of Enoshima, seen in the
background.

We can feel the heat as it affects the main characters: a hat is

removed and a breast is fanned (right); perspiration is wiped from the brow of a sedan-chair carrier, and its occupant smokes a pipe (centre); a sandal is re-tied (left). In the centre, a scantily clad boy from a fishing village draws the attention of the travellers to something happening outside the frame of the print. Down by the shoreline more tourists watch boys swimming and look across towards the shrine gate (torii) and the promise of further refreshment on the island itself.

Hiroshige here pays tribute to Hokusai's Great Wave (p. 16). There is an obvious quote from Hokusai in the wave claws, but this is an attempt at a more naturalistic and less dramatic composition. We are here on the cusp of early Meiji and Victorian art — static waves and over-egged detail with plovers carrying on from the waves. Nature is controlled, made safe and prettified for our gaze. This is set on the Tokaido road, from Edo to Osaka, which often hugs the coast and is washed by stormy seas.

Hiroshige made an earlier set of the Tokaido in the 1830s, which included views of Fuji. Many of his earlier works are more lyrical and atmospheric. He captures the stillness of snow as well as the bustle of shopping streets in Edo, rainstorms and gentle spring breezes, and a boat party watching the moon by a bridge on the Sumida River. This is one of his last works, published posthumously at a time when Japan had begun to open up to the West following Commodore Perry's mission in 1853. Images like this were soon made for foreign consumption as well.

Mount Fuji from the sea at Satta,
Suruga province, colour woodblock print
published in 'Thirty-six views of Mount Fuji', 1859,
by Utagawa Hiroshige (1797–1858).

SHRINES AND TEMPLES were popular destinations for a journey. The motivation was often no more devout than for Chaucer's Canterbury pilgrims in medieval England. The major Shintō shrine at Ise soon developed its own pleasure quarter to deal with its many urban visitors. When the Buddhist image of Kannon was put on display in a Kyoto temple, for example, people abandoned even the cherry blossom to see it. 'Many among them were fashionably dressed ladies; not one of whom seemed to be making the pilgrimage with any thought of the Hereafter. Each showed off her clothes and took such pride in her appearance that even Kannon must have been amused at the sight.' (Ihara Saikaku, *Five Women Who Loved Love*, 1686)

Inari is the Shintō god of rice, and foxes are his messengers. Fushimi Inari Shrine in Kyoto is famous for its many torii gates, built with offerings from worshippers, and one of these is glimpsed here, painted red as usual.

Bunchō, a master of ink painting, brought an idealized, Chinese-based tradition of landscape painting from Kyoto and Osaka to Edo, and combined it with other traditions for his powerful patrons. There is often a sharp edge to his portraits, as can be seen here and in his prints of kabuki onnagata. Very little is known about his life, as for so many Ukiyo-e masters.

Votive painting at the Inari shrine,
by Tani Bunchō (1763–1840).

VISITORS TO SHRINES and temples could also be serious in purpose. This statue reflects the piety of the growing bourgeoisie in cities such as Edo at this time. Although only 40 cm high, the sculpture has considerable power and vividly conveys the serenity and concentration of an elderly lay Buddhist.

There is a tradition throughout Buddhist Asia of lay people, young and old, spending time in monasteries and retreats. They also maintain an active relationship with their local shrines and temples as a regular part of daily life by making offerings, giving food to monks, and visiting regularly to pray and reflect, creating a small oasis of serenity in the midst of the hectic city.

Retired townsman in Buddhist robes,
lacquered wooden sculpture,
late 17th–early 18th century.

Longing for the grass
At the bottom of the pool
Those fireflies

YOSA BUSON (1716–83)

CHOKI WAS ACTIVE from the 1760s to the early 1800s. His work is poetic in atmosphere and recognizable for the serenity of his faces. He shows, like his fellow student Utamaro, how even the typically mask-like face of an Edo beauty can appear alert and interested. This image shows a mother and her small boy (like the young Utamaro) delightedly catching fireflies on a May night, in a garden with irises, flowers which were also a favourite subject for screen painters during this period. Choki also used this kind of mica background for other prints, including one of a very similar beautiful woman watching the sunrise by the sea at New Year. One writer has commented on how Choki's prints may remind us of Modigliani in their elongation of face and figure.

Cool clear water
And fireflies that vanish
That is all there is . . .

CHIYO-NI (1703–75)

Catching fireflies, colour woodblock print with powdered black mica ground, c. 1795, by Eishosai Choki.

HOKUSAI, 'the man mad about drawing', was well known as an eccentric, and was described on his tomb as a 'renowned, original, sincere man'. We have returned at the end of the day to the world of Hokusai's manga (p. 15) and also of his fisherman (p. 19), as well as to his dreamy evocations of land, sea and sky.

Viewing the moon was also an excuse for a boat trip with dinner, for dancing and for poetry. A lady-in-waiting at the imperial court, watching the bright moon, wrote a poem:

> Sadly I see the year is drawing to an end,
> And the night is giving way to dawn,
> While moonbeams wanly shine upon my sleeves.

After another viewing, this time of a starlit night, she was sent a poem by other court ladies:

> Why should we think so fondly of a winter night
> When there was neither moon nor blossoms to be seen?

LADY SARASHINA, *As I Crossed a Bridge of Dreams* (11th century)

Portrait of himself as a fisherman watching the moon, colour woodblock print, 1835, by Katsushika Hokusai (1760–1849).

THE 'FLOWERS OF THE FOUR SEASONS' refers to courtesans in these two volumes of prints by Utamaro. Here we glimpse exhaustion at the end of another day in the Yoshiwara. This artfully cropped and beautifully coloured image is filled with incident: the child is desperate for sleep, one of the women is dozing off while another reads, and a servant puts shutters into place. A whole team of servants were required to provide support for the courtesans; a new generation also had to be trained from a tender age. An entire household might be seen processing through the streets (p. 53).

Mosquito nets are a common theme in Ukiyo-e art, and provide a chance for artists and printmakers to show their skill. One wealthy lady in a novel of the period 'retires to lie at ease in the shelter of an ample mosquito net; and tiny bells tinkle at its corners as the servants fan her, by turns, till she drops off to sleep.'

Retiring for the night under a mosquito net, diptych of colour
woodblock prints, published in 'Picture Book of the Flowers of the
Four Seasons', 1801, by Kitagawa Utamaro (1753–1806).

Princess Takiyasha summons a skeleton spectre to frighten Mitsukuni, triptych of colour woodblock prints, 1844, by Utagawa Kuniyoshi (1797–1861).

GHOSTS AND DEMONS are a popular topic in Japanese art. The master of this genre is Utagawa Kuniyoshi, who has been described as 'the last great master of the Japanese colour print'. In his work beautiful women are attacked by rampaging giant octopuses and carp, or themselves turn into avenging demons; ghosts lurk on the ocean bottom ready to attack the ships of their former enemies. There are bloody suicides, heroes publicly boiled to death in oil, violent explosions in full technicolour – all highly cinematic before their time.

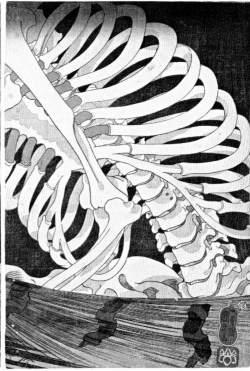

This bravura design is set in the tenth century. The daughter of a defeated warlord is a sorceress, and lives on in the family's ruined palace. In this scene she is trying to frighten to death the warrior Mitsukuni, who has been sent to wipe out the rest of her clan by the men who murdered her father. Despite the appearance of this giant skeleton spectre, he survives and eventually subdues the princess.

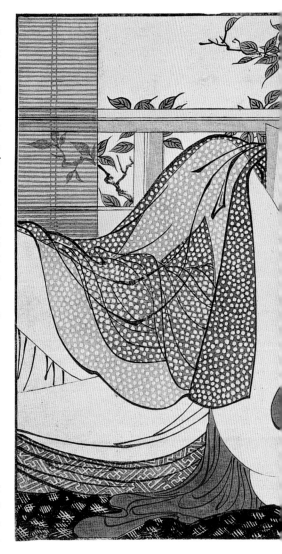

WITHIN the extremely lively tradition of explicit shunga ('spring pictures'), no other artist is as lyrically erotic as Utamaro. In this print he is the master of the understated: the figures are unusually large but we see no faces, just one of the man's eyes; nor is there any explicit activity. Eroticism is in the nape of the woman's neck and the clutching fingers, giving the merest suggestion of what might be happening or about to happen.

The poem on the fan says it all:

Its beak caught firmly
In the clam shell,
The snipe cannot
Fly away
Of an autumn evening

Lovers in an upper room, colour woodblock print published in the album 'Poem of the Pillow', 1788, by Kitagawa Utamaro (1753–1806).

Detail from Ten scenes of lovemaking,
handscroll painting, *c.* 1795–1810,
attributed to Katsukawa Shun'ei (1762–1819).

S HUN'EI SHARPLY characterizes these lovers, but he is hardly more
explicit than the earlier Utamaro on the previous page. In this post-
coital scene the man leans back among the cushions, smoking his pipe.
The woman dozes across his knee, one hand inside her kimono sleeve
pulling it up to slightly cover her face; only her eyebrows and a tightly
closed eye are visible. In other scenes from this scroll a husband surprises
his wife from behind as she washes her hair, and lovers are shown
about to commit suicide. Shun'ei's style has been described as 'excited
and kinetic' in street scenes, actor and sumō prints as well as in these
paintings of lovemaking.

A night like this in the Yoshiwara might begin in the afternoon with eating and drinking, conversation, music and dance before reaching its climax. Utamaro created an album, 'Twelve Hours of the Green Houses', that followed a day in the life of a courtesan as an excuse for a series of ravishing fashion plates. In another of his prints, a courtesan dreams of her wedding, but this was doomed to be a fantasy, for just as 'The standard lie of the prostitute is "I love you", the standard lie of the client is "I will marry you".'

THE ANCIENT Buddhist Mii-dera Temple, by Lake Biwa, was famous for its evening bells, celebrated as one of the three most famous sets of bells in Japan for their plaintive tone. There is an austere grandeur about this print, in which the people are tiny and insignificant as they walk up the road to their destination, drawing the viewer's eye towards the temple in the trees.

The poem reads:

> Lovers think
> 'So begin our
> dawn vows'
> When first they hear
> The evening bell of Mii Temple

Temple bells ring all through Japanese literature, to mark evening and dawn after a sleepless night:

> When the tolling of the temple bell
> Told me that dawn and my vigil's end had come at last,
> I felt as though I'd passed a hundred autumn nights.

> LADY SARASHINA, *As I Crossed a Bridge of Dreams* (11th century)

Evening bell at Mii temple, colour woodblock print, 1834,
by Andō (Utagawa) Hiroshige (1797–1858).

When the floating bridge
Of the dream of a spring night
Was snapped, I awoke:
In the sky a bank of clouds
Was drawing away from the peak.

FUJIWARA NO TEIKA (1162–1241)

THE SUN'S RAYS break over Fuji and a new day begins. Hokusai, by this time in his 70s, has most unusually here introduced Western-style clouds and eliminated any sign of humans. This powerful image varies considerably in colours from one impression to another. Fuji too can adopt many colours, as one medieval writer remembered:

There is no mountain like it in the world. It has a most unusual shape and seems to have been painted deep blue; its thick cover of unmelting snow gives the impression that the mountain is wearing a white jacket over a dress of deep violet.

LADY SARASHINA, *As I Crossed a Bridge of Dreams* (11th century)

Fuji has been sacred since prehistory, and for both Shintō and Buddhist devotees. It is still a challenge for pilgrims to climb, which they often do in order to see the sunrise, and these now include women, who were previously banned. Prints of courtesans in the Yoshiwara sometimes show them viewing Fuji through a telescope: they were virtually imprisoned in the pleasure quarter for their ten years of service.

And the morning after? As one commentator put it:

Mornings the floating world of Yoshiwara sleeps, weary, drugged by sake and other bought pleasures. Along the main street . . . flowering cherry trees scent the morning. The bright blossoms are already falling from the trees, trees that never bear fruit.

South wind, clear sky ('Red Fuji'), colour woodblock print published in 'Thirty-Six Views of Mount Fuji', 1830–33, by Katsushika Hokusai (1760–1849).

ILLUSTRATION REFERENCES

© The Trustees of the British Museum, Department of Asia (JA).

page		page		page	
2	1906.12-10.364(1-3)	37	1906.12-20.1342	68	JP ADD 341-2
9	1937.7-10.68	39	1906.12-10.364(1-3)	71	1906.12-20.220(1)
11	1979.3-5.159, JH 159	41	1907.5-31.390(1-3)	73	1906.12-20.221
13	1912.4-16.220	43	1927.6-13.6	75	1902.2-12.396(25),
15	JP 107	45	1924.3-27.9(1)		JP ADD 1146
16	1937.7-10.147	46	JP 1375	77	1906.12-20.183
19	1937.7-10.162	49	1927.6-13.20	79	1885.12-27.98
21	1907.5-31.204	51	1979.3-5.193	81	1945.11-1.44
22	JP ADD 170-1	53	1979.3-5.193, JIB 515A	83	1906.12-20.479
24	1881.12-10.1434-6	55	1922.12-14.9	85	JP 59
27	1927.6-13.4	57	1979.3-5.146	87	1915.8-23.915-16
29	1907.5-31.490(1-3)	59	1982.6-1.2, JP ADD 687	89	OA+133.6
31	1909.6-18.55	61	1913.5-1.288, JP 1500	91	1980.3-25.4, JP ADD 615
32	1909.6-18.41	63	JP 1588	93	1907.5-31.591
33	1906.12-20.462	65	1907.5-31.622(1-3)	95	1906.12-20.525
35	1906.12-20.1056	67	JIB 90		

QUOTATION SOURCES

(p. 5) Asai Ryoi, 'Tales of the Floating World', R. Lane (trans.), *Images from the Floating World*, OUP, 1978, p. 11; (pp. 8, 18, 80) D. Cobb (ed.), *Haiku*, BMP, 2002, pp. 10, 72, 35; (pp. 8, 17, 38, 40, 69, 76, 94) D. Keene (ed.), *Anthology of Japanese Literature to the 19th Century*, Penguin, 1968, pp. 411, 394, 82, 71, 395, 348, 329, 186; (pp. 82, 94) Lady Sarashina, *As I Crossed a Bridge of Dreams*, I. Morris (trans. and ed.), Penguin, 1975, pp. 111, 39, 57; (p. 95) O. Statler, *All-Japan: The Catalogue of Everything Japanese*, Quill, 1984, p. 197.